Doctor Awad Tarawneh

JORDAN

History culture traditions

Specially produced for:

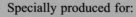

Jordan Distribution Agency Co. Ltd

Published by:

MP GRAPHIC FORMULA
Roma - Italia - 1995

His Majesty Hussein Bin Talal King of Jordan

JORDAN

Up until now Jordan has not been promoted much by the media as a tourist destination due to the fact that the country is geographically situated in the Middle East which is politically quite unstable. In reality, travelling in Jordan not only involves no risk for visitors, because they are protected by the local authorities, but is also a fascinating experience both artistically and culturally.

Jordan is situated in the most privileged place in history, a crossroads on the earliest trade routes and pilgrim paths to Mecca, and has been home to the greatest civilisations of the past. Egyptians, Assyrians, Babylonians, Hittites, Greeks, Romans, Arabs, Turks, Crusaders and the recent English have left traces of their culture in cities which are architectural and artistic treasures.

The whole country has a rich heritage with majestic temples, splendid mosaics, imposing Medioeval castles and historic hillside sites where the Crusaders battled against the Omayyad caliphs.

Moreover, the region is rich in fascinating natural phenomena which include the Dead Sea, in whose waters you will float without any effort whatsoever, and the impressive moon-like visions of the Wadi Rum desert, scene of the famous deeds of Lawrence of Arabia. The desert is still inhabited by Bedouin nomads who are among the most genuine and hospitable people you are likely to meet. It is a fascinating experience to cross the desert on the back of a camel assisted by a local guide.

Scuba diving enthusiasts can explore one of the most beautiful coral reefs in the world.

But the great highlight of a visit to Jordan is the legendary pink city of Petra, built into the living rock of the mountains which have hidden it for centuries from the eyes of the world.

Jordan has developed rapidly in the last century and is able to offer the visitor a range of comfortable modern accomodation, from first class hotels to hostels for young people travelling on a budget.

Geography

Jordan occupies an area of approximately 98,000 sq km and extends from the 29th to the 33th parallel north of the equator and from the 35th to the 38th meridian east of Greenwich. The country borders on the north with Syria, on the south with Saudia Arabia, on the west with Cisjordan (the territories annexed to Jordan in 1950 and now, since the sixday war in 1967, under Israeli occupation) and Israel and on the east with Iraq. There is

access to the Red Sea in the south along the 27 km of coast of the gulf of Aqaba. The borders with Syria, Saudia Arabia and Iraq were marked out after the First World War, following the fall of the Ottoman Empire which had controlled these countries, both politically and militarily. These frontiers were defined in a rather casual way and proof of this is the bizarre bulge along the border with Saudia Arabia known as "Winston's hiccup" about which a legend is told. It is related that this demarcation line was drawn by the English Secretary of State, Churchill, during an attack of the hiccups after a copious meal in Jerusalem in 1920. The first border line with Israel was drawn in 1949, the present one in 1967.

Regions

Jordan may be divided into four main regions. These are the valley of the Jordan river, the Cisjordanian tableland, the Transjordanian tableland and the Desert. The valley of the Jordan river begins in the Lebanon and crosses Jordan from the Syrian border in the north across the Dead Sea as far as Aqaba.

The Jordan river is 251 km long and is fed by the waters of the Tiberiade lake, the river Yarmuk and short tributaries flowing down from the eastern and western tablelands.

The Dead Sea is the deepest depression in the world, 394 m under sea level with a maximum depth of 400m. The famous feature of this sea is the high salt content and it is a place of pluvious origin. The Jordan, as well as other rivers, some of which flow all year round and some only seasonal in the north, flows into the Dead Sea. No vegetation grows around the Dead Sea due to the high salt levels. The Cisjordanian tableland is made up of hills rising to 1000m in height. Long shallow valleys penetrate the western part of the tableland while those descending to the Dead Sea are short and steep.

This is the Holy Land: The Transjordanian tableland extends over the eastern part of the country with highest peaks 1700m above sea level. The central western slope is criss-crossed by wadis – Wadi Zarga, Wadi al Mujib, Wadi al Hesa. Wadi is an Arabic word indicating a valley formed by a watercourse which is dry except during the rainy season. The main urban centres are situated in this area Amman (the capital), Irbid, Jerash Zarga, Madaba, Kerak, Petra and Aqaba.

To the east are the desert steppes which cover two thirds of the country. The desert, which extends as far as Syria, Iraq and Saudia Arabia, is part of the Syrian and Arabian deserts. The landscapes of the Wadi Rum and Wadi Musa, famous also as the "Valley of Moses", are among the most spectacular in the world, on account of their granite and sandstone rock formations. The northeastern part of the desert is composed of vulcanic basalt. The oases scattered here and there are another great attraction. The largest of these is Azraq.

Climate

In summer the weather in the Jordan valley is very hot – daytime temperatures rise above 35°C and reach a maximum of 50°C. Precipitation is scarce. The climate is more reasonable on the Cisjordanian tableland compared to the valley but here too temperatures come close to 35° during the day.

Winters are very short with little rain except in rare years. When cold winds blow, the temperature falls to 7°C.

The weather is fairly similar on the Transjordanian tableland. In the last few years there have been very cold winters in Amman and Petra with heavy snow falls. On the southern part of the tableland the climate is much hotter and drier. The desert region registers extremely high temperatures in summer. The prevailing winds blow from the west and southwest most of the year while in the summer east winds blow as the monsoons approach.

Flora and fauna

The country's vegetation is conditioned by climate and geology. There are three types of landscape; Mediterranean, steppe like and desert. The native vegetation on the tablelands is of the Mediterranean type. There are limited wooded areas with evergreen species in the northwest. The steppes are home to shrubs, artemisias, wild olive trees and splendid flowers such as the Acacia Cyanophilla which can tolerate the long dry periods.

Near the Jordan valley is a place which is a floristic museum – here there are specimens of "Pistacia atlantica" over 1000 years old. The few forests which did exist in Jordan were felled in order to build the Hijaz railway line at the end of the Ottoman period and this has greatly affected the ecological balance. Many of the animal species who once lived in these forests have thus disappeared but some have survived, including the Asiatic jackal, the Arabian fox, the badger, the striped hyena, the wolf and the wildcat. Camels, hares and sand and pyramid rats live in desert regions and wild boar, badgers and goats on the hills

northeast of the Dead Sea. A great variety of birds from all over Europe and the Middle East throng the oases at certain periods of the year. There are also a wide variety of reptiles including different species of iguana, monitor lizards and the Mediterranean chameleon.

The State

The official name of the country is the Hashemite Kingdom of Jordan. It is a constitutional monarchy with a representative government since 1952. The present king is Hussein Bin Talal. The male descendants of the Hashemite dynasty are entitled to succeed to the throne. The next in line is King Hussein's younger brother, Hassan Bin Talal.

The government has executive, legislative and legal functions. Legislative power is entrusted to the National Assembly which has two houses and the king who also has executive power.

The Senate is composed of 40 members elected by the King and the Chamber of Deputies has 80 members, elected every four years by universal suffrage.

The King is invested with full powers. He nominates the Prime Minister and the magistrates whom he may also dismiss, approves cultural amendments, declares war and is the head of the army.

Lastly all laws must be approved by him but his power of veto may be annulled by a majority composed of two thirds of the members of both houses.

Elections should be held every 4 years, but in reality those held in November 1989 were the first since 1967, the year Jordan lost Cisjordan. Since that date martial law has been enforced, today most of the articles have been repealed. The first free elections open to all parties were held on the 8 November 1993 and the results saw the victory of the pro-government candidates and the defeat of opposers to the peace agreements between the PLO and Israel. This victory has had a very postive effect on the country's political stability. The peace agreements were signed in Washington on the 13 September 1993 and were formally recognised by Jordan.

People

The population of Jordan is over 4,000,000. The cities with the greatest number of inhabitants are Amman, Zarga and the surrounding area, El Irbid and Kerak and environs. Most Jordanians are of Arab origin and are descended from the many tribes and clans which came from different areas in different periods. Other minorities are the Circassians from Caucasia, the Chechens and a small group of Armenians.

There are more than 40,000 Bedouins. Originally nomads (bedu means nomad), many have now settled and and no longer travel, growing crops and grazing livestock. Some are semi nomads and move seasonally with their herds in search of pasture. They live in black tents made of goat skins known as *bayt ashsha' ar* "woven hair houses". The Bedouins have played an important role in the history of modern Jordan. From the very beginning they established relations with the Hashemite family and since 1930 represent the principal nucleus of the fighting units in the army. The family is the most important social unit and is patriarchal.

The Palestinians are those who were given Jordanian citizenship after 1948, that is, after the creation of the State of Israel and they form 60% of the Jordanian population.

There is no discrimination between Palestinian refugees and local people. In fact many Palestinians hold important political and economic positions. Despite the fact that the Jordanian government is deeply committed to integrating them within the country, many of them still long to return to an independent Palestine.

UNRAWA, the United Nations agency for help and work, is responsible for aiding refugees and also provides for their education and medical care.

The Circassians arrived in Jordan in the second half of the last century and they settled in Amman, Jerash and Zarga.

Religion

The official religion in Jordan is Islam which literally means submission to the will of Allah. Islam was founded by Mohammed in the VII century. The Koran is the sacred book which contains the dogmas that govern the life of every Moslem: the profession of faith, prayer five times a day, fasting and the pilgrimage to Mecca which every Moslem must make at least once in his or her life. The month of fasting is called Ramadan and it is the ninth in the Moslem calendar. Mohammed's flight from Mecca to Medina in 622 is called the "Hegira" and marks the beginning of the Moslem year.

In Jordan 92% of the population is Moslem.

Islamic minorities are the non Sunnite Moslems, the Circassians and the Chechens. Christians form 6% of the population.

Language

The official language in Jordan is Arabic, side by side with English which is used in the commercial world. There is also a series of dialects. Classical or literary Arabic is used in political and religious dialogue and in the media and has its historical roots in the language in which the Koran was written, maintaining grammar, syntax and vocabulary intact. People speak the Syrio Jordanian dialect. Arabic belongs to the southern group of the Semitic branch of languages. The alphabet contains 28 letters and the short vowels are not written but pronounced. The language is written and read from right to left.

Economy

The Jordanian economy is greatly based on aid from the United States, England and oil-producing Arab countries. The Gulf War inflicted a hard blow on the country, costing over 8 billion dollars.

Today Jordan is committed to overcoming the economic depression and prospects are optimistic. The principal activities in the country are agriculture and livestock rearing.

Agriculture constitutes 10% of GDP and the fundamental problem is the shortage of water. Since 1986 the government has been engaged in an ambitious irrigation project in the semidesert regions of the south, exploiting underground water – bearing strata and constructing dykes, which will provide 20,000 hectares of land for agriculture. Only 6% of land in Jordan is tilled, mainly in the Jordan valley which has a favourable climate and precious water. There are citrus fruit plantations, vineyards and olive and banana groves and tobacco, wheat, barley and beans are grown.

Livestock is mostly sheep, and most other meat has to be imported, and poultry which is sufficient for national requirements.

Jordan has extensive phosphate and potassium deposits in the Wadi Hasa and the Wadi Al Abiad and is the third biggest exporter in the world. There are rich copper and potassium deposits in the Wadi Araba and south of the Dead Sea. These resources have given rise to the only mining activity in the country. The building industry is well developed. Industrial plants are concentrated in the area between Amman and Zarga. The manufacturing industry is still underdeveloped.

Craftwork

The Bedouins are skilled craftsmen and one of their specialities is the production of wool carpets woven on a horizontal loom in bright gaudy colours with natural dyes obtained from desert herbs. The designs are geometric with a great variety of forms. The Bedouins are also skilled at making knives of all shapes and sizes with handles inlaid with gold and silver and semi precious stones.

Other products include glassware, pottery, wood carvings, mother of pearl, traditional coffeepots and glass bottles filled with coloured sand which creates patterns.

Customs and curiosities

One of the most typical Jordanian customs is the marriage rite. Marriages take place between people of the same social rank and the same religious faith and there are still many matches between cousins. The women of the respective families reach an agreement and the young man can visit his future father and mother in law only after obtaining his father's consent and meet his bride only after the official ceremony.

After the agreement between the two families, the young man's relations formally seek the girl's hand. Then the details of the dowry and the caution money in the case of divorce are agreed upon and the wedding date set.

For the wedding feast a tent is decorated with lights and flags where the celebrations last a week. During this period the bridegroom may not see the bride. The feast begins on Monday and ends on Thursday when a cortege of guests accompanies the bride to her new home where the bridegroom awaits her. The following day the relatives of the bridegroom offer the guests a lunch where "MANSAF" is served. This is a traditional dish of boiled meat on a bed of rice flavoured with yogurt and pinenuts.

Then there is the coffee rite which takes place when an agreement is sealed. Coffee is poured until a turn of the cup indicates thank you and the end of the ceremony.

Arabs are fond of exchanging courtesy phrases when they meet and they have a standard repertoire. The most common greeting is "SALAM ALAYKUM" may peace be with you, to which the response is "WA ALAYKUM AS SALAM" and may peace be with you.

In conversation they gesticulate a lot and particular gestures substitute verbal expressions. Raising an eyebrow, moving the head up and down and making a clicking noise with the tongue means "NO", shaking the head from one side to the other "I don't understand", keeping the right hand on the heart when something is being offered "no thank you", turning the hand and giving the wrist a quick tap "what do you want?" or "where are you going?"

To all tourists we say AHLAN WA SAHLAN, WELCOME TO JORDAN.

JERASH

Jerash is a Graeco-Roman city situated 50 km north of Amman. It is known as the "Pompei of the East" due to its extraordinary state of preservation.

The ruins of the ancient city lying in the green well-irrigated valley of Gilaad have always been a great attraction for tourists and archaeologists from all over the world. In the I century BC Jerash belonged to the DECAPOLIS and in this period a forum, theatres and temples were built to embellish the city. During the Byzantine period, the temples were knocked down and churches built in their place.

The entrance to the city is through the imposing ochre-coloured triumphal arch erected in 129 AD to commemorate the arrival of the emperor Hadrian. Beyond the arch is the hippodrome dating from the I-III century AD. It is the largest building in Jerash and could hold up to 15,000 spectators.

The main part of the city is reached through the Rest House which leads to the South Gate, the entrance used by travellers arriving from Amman. Through the gate on the left hand side are the ruins of the temple of Zeus (II century), the forum in an unusual elliptical shape and the southern theatre (I century). From the forum, a colonnaded road leads from the square to the North Gate.

Along this main road towards the north stand the southern tetrapilus, a small shrine with four massive square bases surmounted by four columns each with a statue on top, a group of Omayyad houses and a Nymphaeum (191 AD). A little further on are the vestiges of the only Omayyad mosque in Jerash, built into the atrium of a colonnade in a Roman house. The most imposing building is the Temple of Artemis, dedicated to the goddess who is patron of the city. The area around the temple contains the ruins of numerous churches, all built around 530 AD.

To the east stands the northern theatre, constructed by Diocletian and rebuilt in the fifties.

In the summer an international Festival of Arts and Culture is held in Jerash. The festival lasts ten days and hosts a wide range of cultural activities including painting, music, literature, antiques and theatre.

Below, the South Gate in the Graeco-Roman city of Jerash. On the following page, above, the elliptical Forum, below left, the Cardinus Maximus and right, the Nymphaeum (191 AD).

Above, the Northern Theatre, below and on the following page, the temple of Artemis (Diana).

Above, the Basilica of St Cosma and Damian. Below, a colonnaded street dating from the I century. On the following page, above, the Southern Theatre and below, the imposing triumphal arch built to commemorate the arrival of the Emperor Hadrian

AJLUN

The city of Ajlun is sistuated 22 km west of Jerash and is surrounded by beautiful pine forests and olive groves.

Ajlun is dominated by the beautiful fortress of QUALAT AR-RABAD, dating from the Medioeval period, which stands at a height of 1250 m with a fine view over the Jordan River.

This castle is considered to be the best example of Arab military architecture in the region. It was erected by the Arabs to defend themselves against the Crusaders. In 1260 the fortress was conquered and partly destroyed by the Mongols. In the XVII century it became Ottoman garrison base which was then almost immediately abandoned.

The castle has been partly restored and is in good condition. Along the road which climbs to the fortress is a MOSQUE which was built on the ruins of a Byzantine church and whose square minaret is reputed to be 600 years old.

PELLA

The ruins of Pella are to be found close to the village of TABAQAT-AL FAHL, about 95 km to the north of Amman.

The city was founded in 310 BC by Alexander the Great who made it an important centre of Hellenistic culture.

In Roman times, Pella became one of the ten cities of the Decapolis, a commercial confederation instituted by Pompey.

Christians took refuge here in the II century AD after their flight from Jerusalem. After the Omayyad conquest the city's name was changed to FAHL. A violent earthquake in 747 destroyed the city completely and it was only reconstructed in the XII century by the Mamelukes, to be abandoned once again until the XIX century. Excavations begun in the early seventies have brought to light remains from the Stone Age, vestiges of houses in stone and ceramics, a Bronze Age necropolis and the ruins of the city walls. There are architectonic fragments of a theatre from the I century AD and the ruins of a Byzantine basilica divided into three naves with Corinthian columns and a mosaic floor. Other churches have been found to the west. Recently an Islamic city and a Mameluke mosque from the XIV-XV century were discovered in the Wadi Jirm al-Moz.

UMM QAIS

Situated near Ibrid 500 m above sea level, in a privileged position both for the panoramic views over Lake Tiberiade to the north and the Jordan valley to the south and for its trading links with Syria. Umm Qais is the former Graeco-Roman city of GADARA founded in the IV century BC by Alexander the Great. The city is famous as the birthplace of two literary figures of ancient Greece - the poet Meleagros and the Epicurean philosopher Philodemus.

The city was dominated in turn by the Ptolemaics, the Seleucids, the Romans and the Byzantines up until the Arab conquest in the first half of the seventh century. During the Roman period Pompey made it one of the cities of the DECAPOLIS. The city is divided into two parts, the upper and the lower city.

The lower city on the eastern side still has three Graeco-Roman tombs and two theatres from the same period - the northern theatre and the western theatre. The first is considerably damaged and the second, built in black basalt, is in slightly better shape. Close to the western theatre are the remains of an ancient basilica and a courtyard. In the upper city is the Ottoman village which contains the Rest House and the Archaeological Museum.

The Museum was inaugurated in 1990 and contains works from the Roman period. Further to the west are the remains of the Baths with mosaics, and a Nymphaeum beyond the colonnaded Roman road which cuts the city in two horizontally.

A well-preserved mausoleum and baths were discovered along this road in 1967.

On the previous page, items on display in the Archaeological Museum (below right, the "Goddess of Gadara"). On this page, above, columns in the Forum and below, the Northern Theatre.

UMM el JIMAL

Situated 20 km east of MAFRAG, Umm el Jimal is also known as the "Black city" because it is built in basaltic lava which contrasts with the splendour of Jerash and the other cities of the DECAPOLIS.

The city constitutes one of the best surviving examples of urban settlement in the Roman, Byzantine and Omayyad eras and we can still see traces of the road network, the advanced plumbing system and building techniques. One of the features of the buildings was the system of roofing with long stone shafts.

Umm el Jimal literally means "mother of the camels" and it was founded by the Nabataeans in the I century BC.

Today it is a mass of ruins of houses, churches and Roman barracks surrounded by the remains of the city walls pierced by 7 gates.

THE DESERT CASTLES

These castles were built by the caliphs of the first Omayyad dynasty (VIII century) in the desert area around Amman. Although the Omayyads had made Damascus the capital of their empire, they spent brief periods in the desert to escape from city life, without however giving up the luxuries to which they were accustomed. Here they hunted and raced horses and in the evening organised sumptuous feasts.

For this purpose they built the castles, jewels of ancient Islamic architecture whose roots were in the Graeco-Roman and Byzantine traditions.

The finest examples are in the east of Jordan.

On top of a hill to the northeast of the city of Zarqa stands **Hallabat Castle**. It was built by the Roman emperor Caracalla in the II century AD, as a defence fortress to protect against raids from desert tribes.

In the VII century the castle was transformed into a monastery and in the Islamic era it became the residence of the Omayyad caliphs. Today the castle is a mass of ruined walls and fallen rocks, some of which bear Greek inscriptions.

AMRA CASTLE

About 35 km southeast of Amman is the small **Amra Castle** which was built during the reign of the Caliph Walid 1 (705-715). It is the best preserved of the desert castles. The interior is beautifully frescoed and the floors are covered in mosaics. A feature of these frescoes is the representation of human figures which is prohibited by Islam. The dome is decorated with the constellations of the Zodiac.

On this page and on the previous one, some of the splendid frescoes inside the Castle.

AZRAQ CASTLE

A little over 100 km to the east of Amman stands the Roman-Islamic fort of **Azraq** built in black basalt. It was erected during the Roman period and rebuilt in 1236-37. The heavy monolithic doorways and bas reliefs with animal and plant motifs date from the time of the Romans. Of interest is the system of roofing in some rooms which uses stone slabs rather than wood.

KARANAH CASTLE

The mysterious **Karanah Castle** is located about 60 km from Amman and was built in pink brick on a square ground plan with towers on all corners and in the middle of each side. It is the only castle which was built for defence purposes. We do not know the exact date of construction. The castle is still intact.

MUSHATTA CASTLE

Mushatta Castle is situated in an arid stony desert 35 km from Amman and close to the airport.
It is considered to be the largest and most gorgeous of the Omayyad castles but for some unknown reason it was never finished.
Today nothing remains of the former magnificence. Fragments of stuccowork, mosaics and marble floors give an idea of what the original castle was like.
The great brick vaults are an extaordinary feature of this building.

KAN ZAMAN

This is the former house of ABU-GIABER, a Jordanian gentleman who offered date and butter cakes free of charge to travellers arriving from inland.

The house stands on the "TEL" hill outside Amman to the south. KAN ZAMAN means "once upon a time" in Arabic and in fact the turn of the century architecture in the town centre evokes the way of life in small Jordanian towns of that period.

Within the central area are a series of corridors with small craft workshops and a restaurant where typical Arab dishes are served and guests can enjoy a belly dancing show.

Today it is an important handcraft centre producing pottery, jewellery, carpets and bottles filled with coloured sand.

On these pages, some typical crafts in this village famous for traditional handcrafts and a type of architecture which evokes the way of life in the last century in small Jordanian towns.

AMMAN

Amman is the ancient and modern capital of Jordan, an active commercial and administrative centre with more than one million inhabitants.

From 1200 BC onwards it was the Ammonite capital RABAT AMMON and then the Graeco-Roman city of Philadelphia.

The city originally spread out on 7 "hills", now there are more than 19. The heart of the city centre is the al-Hussein mosque built in 1924.

The main hill is Jebel Ammon where all the embassies and the most prestigious hotels are located.

Amman is a city of many contradictions, ancient and modern live side by side - Bedouins in typical headress, the "MENDIL" with the "IGAA'L", mingle with businessmen in classic Western clothes. In this mainly modern city there are many monuments worth visiting. The ruins of the citadel on the top of the Jebel al Qala witness the long history of this site. There are ruins of Roman, Byzantine and Moslem buildings, including vestiges of the Temple of Hercules erected at the time of the emperor Marcus Aurelius, and the imposing National Archaeological Museum known today as the QASR 'palace', with the remains of a Byzantine basilica nearby. Many important monuments may be seen from the old city of Philadelphia including the Roman THEATRE (II century AD) with 6,000 seats, the NYMPHAEUM, a monumental fountain from the II and III centuries AD, now surrounded by modern buildings which hide the decorated facade, the ODEON (II century) a small theatre for musical performances with a capacity of 500 and the Forum, the main square once limited on three sides by a portico supported by Corinthian columns.

The modern district has grown enormously in the last decades especially from north to south and towards the west.

The imposing blue-tiled dome of the modern mosque al-MALlK ABDULLAH, completed in 1990, can be seen from many points in the city.

Another mosque stands south of the Jebel al-Qala on top of the Jebel al-Ashrafiyah, the highest and steepest Jebel in Amman. It is the ABU-DARWISH MOSQUE, built in black and white stone placed in alternate rows. The very modern al Hussen ar-Riyadiyah medina, "sports city" was inaugurated in 1971 in a verdant area of the city. There are excellent sports facilities,meeting places and a palace of arts and culture.

Amman has also a prestigious university which organises Arab language courses for foreign students. Inside a museum has been created which displays manufactured articles from the Bronze and Iron ages.

On the previous page, the Roman Theatre, situated in the old district of Amman. On this page, above, two of the extremely fine mosaics housed in the Museum of Popular Traditions. Below, reconstruction of a scene from Bedouin daily life in the Folklore Museum.

On this page, above left, small statues of Aphrodite, right, an example of Nabataean art and below, anthropoid sarcophagi, on display in the Archaeological Museum. On the following page, the remains of the imposing Temple of Hercules, built during the reign of Marcus Aurelius (161-180).

Above, the ruins of the Byzantine Church, below, the Omayyad Castle, both situated on the hill of the citadel. On the following page the interior of the Omayyad Castle.

Above left, the Great Mosque. Below, and on the following page, the Al Ashrafiyia Mosque.

Above, the Hussein sports centre, below, a modern district in Amman. On the previous page, the King Abdullah Mosque.

IRAQ AL-AMIR

Situated in the fertile valley of the Wadi Ser and 20 km west of Amman, Iraq al-Amir means the prince's caves and consists of a series of caves laid out like an amphitheatre.

The place is famous for the ruins of the QASR al-ABD, castle of the slaves, probably dating from the II century BC, home to the Tobiad family. The Castle originally stood in the centre of an artificial lake but seismic phenomena have altered the structure. The building has a rectangular base with four corner towers and is built in enormous blocks of white stone of about 20 tons, the only example in the entire Middle East.

Just recently a French team of experts finished restoring the castle to its original state.

THE DEAD SEA

This large salt lake situated 400m under sea level was called the Dead Sea by the Crusaders but the local place name is "AL-BAHR AL-MAYIT" or "BAHR LUT" (the sea of Lot). The sea is 55 km from Amman and the journey is particularly scenic. At sunset the sun's rays seem like fiery swords cleaving the surrounding mountains.

Sparkling pearly rocks emerge from the water and create a fairytale atmosphere. The name speaks for itself, the sea is devoid of life due to the high concentration of salts and minerals which have the power to heal all types of skin disease and which were already famous at the time of Herod the Great. The mud on the beaches has the same healing powers.

There is a clinic here and therapeutic baths as well as a pleasure craft harbour, sports centres and a comfortable hotel for visitors.

The water is always warm but it is impossible to go underwater. A bather always stays on the water's surface and it is not surprising to see people sitting afloat in the water and reading the newspaper. On the southern coast, the Jordanians have begun to extract potassium which is refined in plants south of Safi.

44

MADABA

Madaba is a small town situated on a hillside about 30 km south of AMMAN and easily reached along the king's road.

The town is famous for its splendid Byzantine mosaics which are found in churches and public and private buildings and it is for this reason that the town is called the "city of mosaics".

Historically, Madaba is the biblical Maobite city of MEDABA. At different times it was under the dominion of the Israelites. In 63 AD it became a Roman colony and in this period was a very prosperous city which continued to flourish under the Byzantines and the Omayyads. Most of the mosaics date from this period. The Roman and Byzantine mosaics reached their artistic peak between the II and V century AD. The city's decline began in 614 when it was destroyed by the Persians and progressively abandoned. It was only at the end of the nineteenth century that it was repopulated by Christian Arab tribes.

The Mosaics

The distinctive feature of the Madaba mosaics is the detail in each design. Plants and animals are the predominate motifs. The plants chosen are generally symbolic and include acanthus leaves, vines and country scenes.

The most precious mosaics are kept in the Greek Orthodox Church of St George and in the Church of the Holy Apostles.

The famous mosaic of the "MAP OF PALESTINE", the oldest map of the Holy Land which dates from the VI century AD, can be seen in the Church of St George.

Of great interest too is the ARCHAELOGICAL MUSEUM which houses gold ornaments and other items from the Roman period, fragments of mosaic floors and a vast collection of antique jewellery and coins. Recent archaeological excavations have uncovered a paved Roman road.

In 1991 a school of restoration for the mosaics was inaugurated. Madaba is also famous for the production of brightly coloured woollen carpets.

Below, the city of Madaba. On the previous page above, landscapes around the Dead Sea, below, the outskirts of the city.

Above left, a copy of the Mesha Stele and below, other items on display in the Madaba Museum.
On the following page, above, a mosaic depicting the Sacrifice of Christ and below, a small statue of Venus.

47

Mosaics of the map of Palestine housed in the Greek Orthodox church in Madaba.

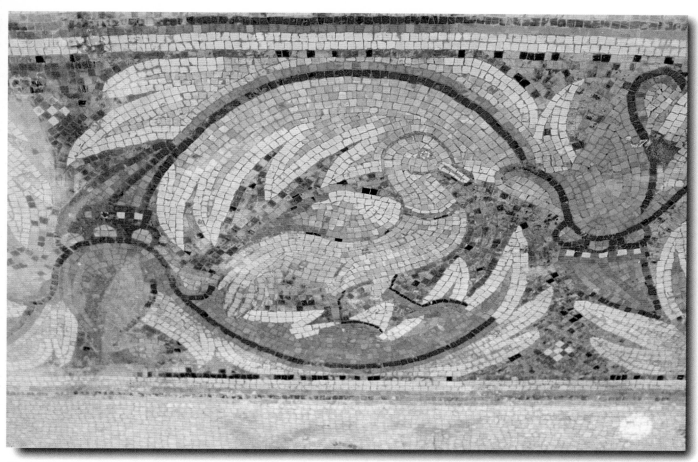

On this page and on the following one, mosaics in the Church of the Holy Apostles in Madaba.

MOUNT NEBO

Mount Nebo rises on the western extremity of the ABARIM tableland about 100 km to the west of Madaba.

Mount Nebo (Gebel Nebo) is 802 m high with a splendid view embracing the valley of the Jordan and the Dead Sea, and on a clear day as far as Jerusalem. It is a solitary hill exposed to all winds and is thought to be the site of the tomb of Moses. Excavations by the Franciscan fathers from 1930 onwards have revealed the ruins of a church and a monastery. The Church was built in the IV century and then enlarged in Byzantine times. Little remains of the architecture but the well preserved mosaic floor can still be seen in a building erected by the friars to protect the ruins.

Below, the entrance to the Church in Mount Nebo, above right, a mosaic inside.

On these two pages and on the following one some views of the Mount Nebo Basilica.

AL MUKHAYYAT

The village of KHIRBAT AL MUKHAYYAT lies near Mount Nebo and some writers believe that the present city occupies the original site of the city of Nebo mentioned in the Bible.

We know for certain that in the V century the city had a Christian population but the finding of tombs dating from the II century BC allows us to assume that the city was inhabited even earlier.

Archaeological excavations in 1990 in the Church of SS Lot and Procopius have brought to light an extremely fine mosaic in an excellent state of preservation. There is another mosaic in St George's Church.

MKAWER (MACHAERUS)

This village is situated less than 40 km south of Amman, at the foot of a hill 700 m high, on which stand the ruins of the massive walls of the fortress of MACHAERUS (today Muquawir). This is where John the Baptist was beheaded by Herod in order to maintain his promise to beautiful Salomè.

This fortress was built by Herod the Great around the year 100 BC in order to control the Nabataeans and was totally destroyed during the Roman siege.

From the ruins of the fortress there is a fine view as far as the Dead Sea and the hills surrounding Jerusalem.

AR RABBA

Situated 100 km to the south of Amman and 20 km from Kerak, the small town of Ar Rabba lies on the King's Road.

The town was originally Ar Moab, mentioned in the Bible with regard to the exodus of the Israelites.

Two Corinthian columns, a Byzantine church and a Roman temple can still be seen among the ruins of the ancient city. The Roman temple is almost intact and contains inscriptions dedicated to Diocletian, in the niche to the left of the entrance, and to Maximian, in the right hand niche (III century AD).

On the previous page, two views of the Macheron hill. On this page, right, the capital of a column in the archaelogical site in Ar Rabba and, below, the King's Road.

On these two pages, views of Ar Rabba.

KERAK

The city of Kerak is often mentioned in the Bible by the name KIR CARESET and was the ancient capital of the kingdom of Moab.

The city is situated on the ancient caravan routes which nearby linked Egypt and Syria at the time of the biblical kings and were later reused by the Greeks and the Romans. The arrival of the Crusaders strengthened the city's position. In 1142, King Baldwin ordered the construction of the Kerak fortress to defend the strategic position of the city, halfway between Aqaba and Jerusalem. This fort is part of a series of fortifications built by the Crusaders along a line running from the Dead Sea along the King's road to Aqaba and as far as northern Turkey. In 1176, the city became part of the domain of REGINALD of CHANTILLON, a Crusader knight, notorious for his cruelty. He killed his enemies by throwing them from the castle ramparts at a height of 500m above ground level.

In 1189 the city was taken by Saladin, then it passed to the Turks and subsequently the fortress was abandoned but not the city itself which continued to prosper.

The old city was surrounded by walls still standing plan and contains a warren of rooms and passageways with vaulted roofs.

Transversally there are two moats, one on the north side to separate the fortress from the city, the other on the south side larger than the first. The latter separates the citadel from the rise 20 m higher again which could have permitted an enemy to dominate the stronghold. On the western side the castle has two boundary walls, one outer, one inner.

The castle was built with different materials which allow us distinguish the parts built by the Crusaders and those constructed later by the Moslems. The former used an extremely hard vulcanic rock coloured dark red and black and the latter a soft grey or yellow limestone cut into regular blocks.

It is still possible to see the cisterns. A series of steps leads to the Museum which houses utensils from the Neolithic period and earthenware items from the Bronze and Iron Ages as well as one of the copies of the MESHA STELE and the translation of its inscription.

Above, the ruins inside the Kerak fortress. Below and on the following page, two views from the Castle.

SHOBAK

Shobak is situated halfway between KERAK and PETRA on the central hills of Jordan called ASH SHARA'.

On one of these hillsides stands the "MONS REALIS" fortress built by Baldwin 1, King of Jerusalem, in 1115. The fortress was attacked many times by Saladin who finally succeeded in capturing it in 1189.

In the XIV century it was restored by the Mamelukes but today all that remains of the original structure are the outside walls with one tower bearing inscriptions in Arabic, while the interior is badly damaged. Inside the fortress there are two churches from the period of the Crusades, a deep well with 365 steps hewn out of the rock, which served as a secret passage, bathrooms, cisterns and conduits for rain water.

On the walls there are Arab inscriptions dating from the time of Saladin.

On these pages views of Shobak Castle and the surrounding area.

PETRA

The city of Petra, which in Greek means rock, is the principal attraction in Jordan. It is situated about 262 km south of Amman and is also known as the "PINK CITY" thanks to the particular colour of the city at dawn and at dusk.

Over 2,000 years ago Petra was the capital city of the Nabataeans, Bedouins originally from northern Arabia. In 106 AD the city was conquered by the Romans who left many traces of their way of life. They built a colonnaded street, public baths and many other fine buildings. With the advent of Christianity, the city became a bishop's see. In the VII century Petra was captured by the Moslems and lost its importance as capital of a flourishing empire that it had enjoyed under the Nabataeans. Following the Crusades in the XII century, the city regained some of that former importance but after this brief period it remained hidden and forgotten until the XIX century, known only to the Bedouin nomads in the area who still live there today. Much of the charm of the city is due to its location on the edge of the "WADI MUSA", with steep sandstone mountains where the town of the same name stands. Here is the "AYN MUSA" (Moses' spring), a small building with three white domes where it is related that water began to flow from the place where Moses struck the rock.

Descending towards the West, the visitor arrives at the REST HOUSE where entrance tickets may be bought and horses and guides hired to cross the SIQ which leads to the KHAZNEH. The SIQ is an immense split in the rocky mountain about 1km long. The walls of this winding gorge are about 100 m high and at some points it seems almost as if they are touching at the top.

The KHAZNEH (treasure) is so called because of a legend relating that a pharaoh hid his treasure here. Some believe it to be the tomb of a Nabataean king and some that it is the temple of Isis. It is however the most attractive monument in the city, carved in rocky sandstone. The final scene of the film "Indiana Jones" was filmed here.

On the way down to the city there are hundreds of magnificent monuments carved out of the rock itself, including temples, beautiful royal tombs, a Roman amphitheatre which could hold 8,000 spectators, funeral chambers, banqueting halls, acquaducts, cisterns, imposing stairways, baths, a Roman style colonnaded street, markets, places of worship and sacrificial altars.

Below, the tomb of the Obelisks and, on the facing page, the entrance to the Siq. On the following pages, a Nabataean tomb in the Siq and El Khazneh (the Treasury).

Above, the Theatre, below, a view of the Royal Tombs. On the following page the tomb of the Urn.

Above, the internal chamber in the tomb of the Urn. Below left, the Sesto Florentinus Tomb and right, the Silk Tomb. Facing page the Corinthian tomb.

Above the Palace tomb and, below, a general view of the Royal Tombs.

Above, monumental gate with three arches, below, El Bint Castle.

On this page the Nabataean Museum and various items on display. On the previous page, above, the Turkmaniya tomb and, below, a craftsman at work creating a bottle filled with coloured sand.

Above, the Monastery, below, a panoramic view of the surrounding area. On the previous page, the tomb of the Lion.

Above, the High Sacred Place, below, the interior of the Triclinium tomb. Facing page, the path leading to the High Sacred Place.

WADI RUM

The Wadi Rum desert is also known as the "Valley of the Moon" because of the surreal nature of the landscape.

The Wadi's fame is linked to the adventures of Lawrence of Arabia who crossed it on his way to conquer Aqaba. The area has been immortalised in the frames of the famous film by David Lean which tells the true story of the exploits of the British colonel. The Wadi Rum takes its name from "WADI" which means the bed of a former river which has dried up, surrounded by towering sandstone mountains looming up from great expanses of white and pink sand. Today the wadi is home to numerous Bedouin tribes who have lived there for centuries.

At the entrance to the Wadi Rum is a fortress belonging to the DESERT POLICE whose only form of transport is by camel, "the desert ship".

Close to the REST HOUSE lie the ruins of a Nabataean temple consacrated to the god DUSHARA (70-106 AD) of which only the foundations remain. About 800 m from the temple is the AYN ASH SHALLALAH spring also known as "Lawrence's fountain". An even more beautiful stream is hidden at the end of the Jebel RUM, only 500 m from the rest house and this is the largest of all those to be found in the area. A preIslamic cemetery from the III-IV century BC has recently been discovered. It contains many funeral stones both carved and with portraits.

The best way to explore the desert is on foot, by camel or by jeep. Excursions in the mountains are also possible.

On these pages and on the next two, views of the Wadi Rum.

AQABA

Aqaba is situated on the transparent waters of the Red Sea and is surrounded by mountains which change colour according to the time of day. Just a few metres from the sandy beaches lies an enchanting underwater world containing coral, plants and brightly coloured fish which can be visited by simply diving under.

The mild climate even during the winter months and the magnificent setting on the gulf of the same name make this city one of the main tourist centres in Jordan and an important mercantile port. The coastline is well supplied with excellent hotels and restaurants and water sports centres offering a variety of sports, including fishing, waterskiing, sailing and windsurfing.

History

The history of Aqaba begins in the V century BC and the city can probably be identified with the biblical city EZION JEBER mentioned in the Old Testament.

The city's role as a mercantile port goes back to the time of King Solomon and the Queen of Sheba (I millenium BC) who founded sea trading activities based on the rich natural resources of the region-gold, spices and precious stones. The city was conquered by the Edomites (VIII century BC), by the Nabataeans (II century BC) and the Roman Empire in 106 AD.

In the VII century it became the Moslem city of Ayla and a crossing point for pilgrims on their way to the holy cities Islam. The city was occupied by the Crusaders, the Mamelukes, whose Sultan constructed Aqaba Fort south of the coastline, and the Ottomans who were driven out during the First World War by Prince Faisal and a group of Bedouins. The Hashemite coat of arms above the main entrance to the fortress dates from this last period.

In 1925 the city was incorporated into Transjordan and in 1954 it became Jordan's harbour. In 1965 King Hussein ceded 6,000 sq km of the Jordan desert to Saudia Arabia in exchange for 12 km of coast to make the beautiful YAMANIEH barrier reef Jordanian territory and increase the activity of the port.

The Archaeological Museum close to the castle contains interesting exhibits from the various epochs of the city's history and is well worth a visit. There is also an Acquarium which houses many different species of marine animals.

Individual and group trips in glass bottomed boats to admire the beauty of the undergound world are organised from the beaches.

Aqaba is also the headquarters of many European scuba diving clubs which hold skindiving courses here.

To complete a stay in this city the visitor can travel to Pharaoh Island, which is regularly linked to Aqaba, where there is a Crusader castle from the XII century.

Below, the Gulf of Aqaba. On the following page, above, the Abu Daoud Mosque. Below left, the Fort, right, the Minaret of an ancient Mosque.

The Aqaba acquarium contains brightly coloured fish belonging to species living in the waters of the Gulf.

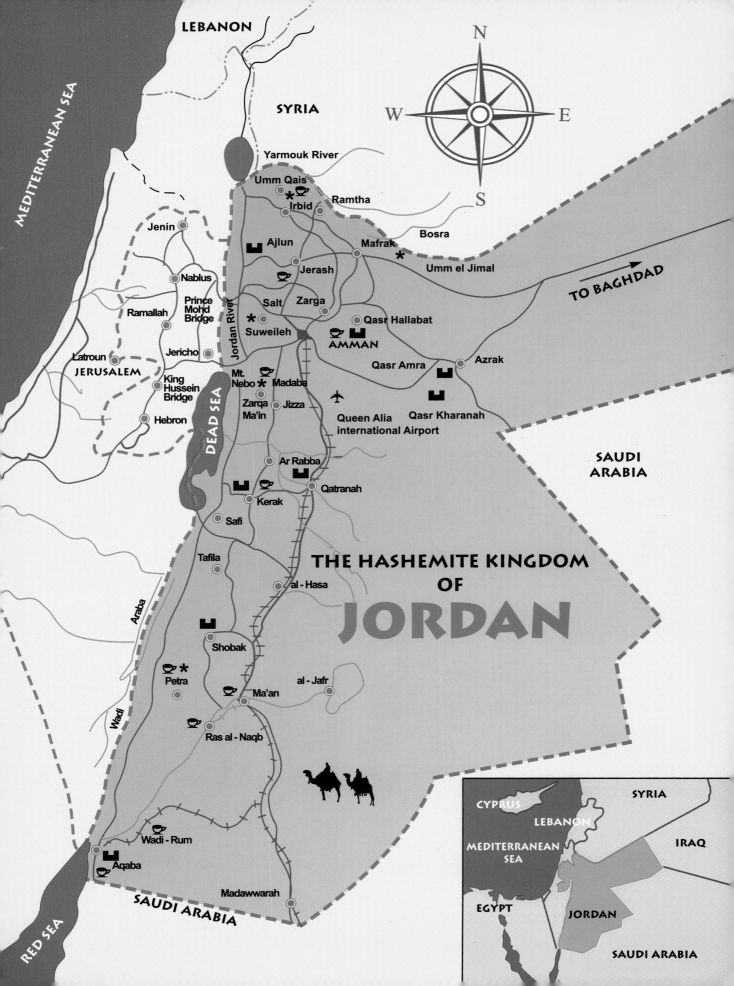

Index

Sole distributor:

Jordan Distribution Agency Co. Ltd.

P.O. Box 375 Tala't Jabal Amman - Amman Jordan
Tel. +962 +6 +630191-2
Fax: +962 +6 +635152

Ministry of Information authorization N. 301/5/1995
Deposit N. 433/5/1995

© Photographs by Bruna Polimeni
Cover design by Enzo Sferra

Printed in Italy by Grafica Di Leo S.r.l. Rome